ZURICH TRAVEL GUIDE 2023 - 2024

Experience The Best of Zurich: A Complete Pocket Guide Book to Unlock The Hidden Gems, Top Attractions and Etiquettes of Switzerland

BY

WILLIAM JOSE

ZURICH
TRAVEL GUIDE 2023 - 2024
William Jose

TABLE OF CONTENTS

INTRODUCTION

Zurich is Switzerland's biggest city and the country's economic, cultural, and financial hub. Zurich is located in northern Switzerland, near the northwestern extremity of Lake Zurich, and is surrounded by gorgeous landscapes and the Swiss Alps. With a 2,000-year history, Zurich has grown into a dynamic and international city while retaining its historic beauty. It is well-known for its good living standards, fast public transit, cleanliness, and scenic surroundings.

Zurich is a significant worldwide financial and banking center, and it is home to the headquarters of various multinational banks and financial organizations. The city's economy is broad, including medicines, machinery, textiles, and tourism. It is also a prominent research and innovation hub, with several notable universities and research organizations.

Zurich has a diverse choice of cultural attractions and activities. With various galleries, museums, and theaters, the city has a strong arts culture. Among the city's cultural institutions are the Kunsthaus Zurich, the Swiss National Museum, and the Rietberg Museum.

Zurich is also well-known for its shopping, with Bahnhofstrasse, one of the world's most elite shopping districts, dotted with luxury shops and landmark stores. The city is a foodie's paradise, with a diversified culinary scene that caters to all tastes and budgets. There is something for every appetite, from traditional Swiss food to cosmopolitan specialties.

Outdoor lovers can also find much to do in Zurich. Beautiful scenery surrounds the city, including Lake Zurich and the adjoining Uetliberg mountain, which provides trekking and panoramic views of the city and the Alps. Within the city, transportation is good, with an efficient public transit system that includes trams, buses, and trains. Zurich Airport is one of Europe's busiest and offers great connections to locations all over the globe.

Overall, Zurich is a city that blends natural beauty, cultural depth, and economic vigor in a seamless manner. Zurich offers something for everyone, whether you're interested in history, art, finance, or just enjoying the magnificent Swiss environment.

Brief Historical Background Of Zurich

Human habitation in the Zurich area dates back to the Paleolithic epoch, demonstrating an early link to the region. Zurich, on the other hand, started to develop as a prominent colony during the Roman period. In the first century AD, the Romans erected a customs station known as Turicum, taking advantage of its strategic position along major trade routes.

Zurich fell under the power of the Alemanni, a Germanic tribe, after the collapse of the Western Roman Empire. It became a part of the Carolingian Empire, and then the Holy Roman Empire, in the ninth century. Zurich grew in significance as a religious center during this period, with the building of various monasteries and the establishment of the Grossmünster cathedral.

Zurich joined the Swiss Confederation, a loose coalition of autonomous states, in the 13th century. The city eventually achieved autonomy and positioned itself as a key member of the confederation, defining Swiss politics and affairs. Because of its profitable commerce, notably in textiles and financial services, Zurich's wealth and prominence rose fast throughout the Late Middle Ages.

Zurich was greatly influenced by the Protestant Reformation in the 16th century. Huldrych Zwingli, a prominent reformer, spoke here, contributing to the city's conversion to Protestantism in 1524. The Reformation resulted in substantial social, cultural, and economic upheavals, and Zurich gained a reputation as a center of intellectual and theological discussion.

Throughout the years that followed, Zurich thrived as a center of industry, education, and innovation. The city experienced industrialization and urbanization in the nineteenth century, with the rise of manufacturing, banking, and the textile sector. This century also saw the emergence of prestigious educational institutions such as the University of Zurich.

Zurich cemented its status as a worldwide financial hub throughout the twentieth century, attracting foreign enterprises and becoming home to several multinational corporations. The city also played an important role in diplomatic endeavors and housed a number of international organizations, which contributed to its reputation as a cosmopolitan and multicultural metropolis.

Zurich is currently a prosperous city known for its great quality of life, beautiful natural surroundings, and lively arts and culture scene. It is still a significant global financial hub, with a focus on sustainable development and innovation. Zurich's historical heritage is visible in its well-preserved medieval old town, architectural sites, and museums, enabling tourists to immerse themselves in its intriguing history while still enjoying the contemporary conveniences of a vibrant 21st-century metropolis.

Zurich's Population and Ethnic Groups

Zurich, Switzerland's biggest city, is known for its rich cultural variety and dynamic population of around 432,000 people, making it the most populated city in the country.

Zurich is an ethnic melting pot, with a varied mix of individuals from different origins and nations. Because of its economic success, high quality of life, and robust job market, the city has long been a popular destination for immigrants. As a result, Zurich boasts a sizable number of foreign nationals who have made the city their home.

The official languages of Switzerland are German, French, Italian, and Romansh. Swiss German, a dialect of German unique to the area, is the major language spoken in Zurich. However, because of the city's international orientation, English is frequently understood and used, notably in the business and tourist sectors.

Zurich's population includes both Swiss citizens and people from other countries. Expatriates from nearby European nations such as Germany, France, and Italy make up a significant component of Zurich's foreign population. Furthermore, the city attracts professionals from all over the globe, including skilled workers, researchers, and professors.

Zurich is also home to several ethnic and cultural populations. Balkan, Turkish, and Portuguese immigrants have formed substantial populations in the city. With a range of cultural events, festivals, and foreign food accessible across the city, the presence of these varied populations adds to Zurich's global ambiance.

Zurich's municipal administration and numerous organizations put a high value on encouraging integration and inclusion among its citizens. Efforts are being undertaken to enhance social cohesiveness and cultural interchange among various ethnic and cultural groupings.

Finally, Zurich is a global city with a wide population of nations and races. Its diversity and international character add to Zurich's lively and dynamic environment, making it an appealing destination to live, work, and visit.

Zurich Climate

Zurich has four different seasons: spring, summer, autumn, and winter.

Here is a basic summary of Zurich weather over the various seasons:

Spring (March to May): Zurich's spring is distinguished by warm temperatures. Temperatures in March vary from roughly 1°C (34°F) to 10°C (50°F). Temperatures in May may range from 10°C (50°F) to 20°C (68°F). However, spring weather may be unpredictable, with rain showers on occasion.

Summer (June to August): Summers in Zurich are often pleasant and warm. Temperatures vary from 18°C

(64°F) to 25°C (77°F) on average. The hottest months are July and August, with temperatures sometimes topping 30°C (86°F). Summer is also the wettest season, with thunderstorms and rains on occasion.

Autumn (September to November): Temperatures in Zurich gradually fall over the autumn season. Temperatures in September might still be in the 15°C (59°F) range. Temperatures vary from 2°C (36°F) to 10°C (50°F) by November. During this season, rainfall rises, particularly in October and November.

Winter (December to February): Zurich's winters are chilly, with temperatures often falling below freezing. The coldest months are December and January, with average temperatures ranging from -2°C (28°F) to 4°C (39°F). Snowfall is typical in the winter, and the city may endure extended periods of snow cover.

Zurich's Religious Practice

Zurich, Switzerland's biggest city, offers a diversified religious environment with a broad diversity of religious activities. Here are some of the most important faiths and religious activities in Zurich:

Christianity is the prevalent religion in Zurich, with the majority of the inhabitants identifying as Roman Catholic or Protestant. The city's ancient churches, such as the Zurich Minster (Grossmünster) and St. Peter's Church, draw both visitors and residents for worship and religious ceremonies.

Islam: Zurich's Muslim community is rising, and the city contains many mosques and Islamic institutes. The Islamic Cultural Center of Zurich is Zurich's biggest mosque, serving as a center for the Muslim population and providing prayer facilities, Islamic education, and community activities.

Judaism: Zurich has a long history of Jewish presence, and the city boasts a vibrant Jewish community. The Zurich Synagogue, situated in the Old Town, is the Jewish community's primary site of prayer. Religious services, cultural activities, and educational programs are held in the synagogue.

Hinduism: Zurich has a Hindu community, and followers may worship their beliefs in Hindu temples across the city. The Sri Ganesha Temple, dedicated to Lord Ganesha, is a famous temple that serves as a spiritual and cultural hub for Zurich's Hindu population.

Buddhism: There are many Buddhist institutions and meditation groups in Zurich where people may practice Buddhism and learn about its teachings. The Buddhist Center Zurich and the Tibet Institute Rikon are two of the city's most famous Buddhist organizations, both of which provide meditation sessions, lectures, and seminars.

Different faiths: Aside from the faiths listed above, Zurich is a varied city that accepts a variety of different religious traditions. Smaller Christian denominations, such as Orthodox Christianity and Evangelical Free Churches, as well as smaller groups representing Sikhism, the Bahá' Faith, and other religious systems, fall into this category.

While Zurich has a diverse religious landscape, Switzerland as a whole is noted for its dedication to religious freedom and tolerance. Religions of various faiths are typically allowed to practice without prejudice or limitation.

Air Travel To Zurich : Countries And Price Rates

The cost of traveling to Zurich from various countries might vary based on variables such as distance, time of year, airline, and flight availability. Here are some examples of flights from other countries, along with their estimated prices (round-trip rates in USD):

London, United Kingdom: Round-trip tickets may cost between $100 and $300, depending on the airline and purchasing period.

Paris, France: A round-trip ticket to Paris will cost between $150 and $400, depending on the airline and season.

New York : Round-trip tickets from New York City to Zurich may vary from $500 to $1,200, depending on the airline, layovers, and booking time.

Dubai, United Arab Emirates: Round-trip prices may range from $400 and $1,000, depending on the airline, layovers, and booking period.

Tokyo, Japan: Round-trip tickets from Tokyo to Zurich may cost anywhere between $600 and $1,500, depending on the airline, layovers, and booking time.

Sydney, Australia: A round-trip flight from Sydney to Zurich will cost between $900 and $1,800, depending on the airline, layovers, and booking time.

Land Travel to Zurich : Countries And Price Rates

Here are some examples of how to get to Zurich by land from several countries, along with estimated expenses. Please keep in mind that these rates are subject to change and may vary based on the time of year, method of transportation, and other considerations. It's always a good idea to confirm the most recent information with the relevant transportation companies.

From Germany:

Rail: Several German cities have direct rail connections to Zurich. Prices vary based on the departure city and train type. A second-class ticket from Munich to Zurich, for example, may cost between €40 and €70.

Bus: Companies such as FlixBus provide trips from several German cities to Zurich. Prices range from €15 and €30, depending on distance and prior booking time.

From France:

Train: TGV trains link major French cities to Zurich. A second-class ticket from Paris to Zurich, for example, may cost between €70 and €120.

Bus: Several bus companies, including FlixBus and Eurolines, provide trips from several French cities to Zurich. Prices might vary from €25 and €70, depending on the departure city and distance traveled.

From Italy:

Rail: Direct rail connections exist from Italian cities such as Milan and Venice to Zurich. A second-class ticket might cost between €30 and €100, depending on the departing city and kind of train.

Bus: Companies such as FlixBus and Eurolines provide trips from several Italian cities to Zurich. Prices range from €20 and €70, depending on distance and prior booking time.

From Austria:

Rail: There are direct rail connections from Austrian cities such as Vienna and Salzburg to Zurich. Prices vary based on the departure city and train type. A second-class ticket from Vienna to Zurich, for example, might cost between €50 and €100.

Bus: FlixBus and Eurolines provide bus service from many Austrian cities to Zurich. Prices might vary from €15 and €50, depending on distance and prior booking time.

These are just a few examples; there are several additional alternative paths to Zurich from other nations. It is best to check with transit providers, such as railway companies or bus operators, for the most up-to-date timetables and pricing.

Is it Possible To Go By Sea to Zurich?

It is not feasible to go by water to Zurich. Zurich is located in Switzerland's landlocked nation, deep inland, distant from any large bodies of water. Lake Zurich is the nearest big body of water to Zurich, however it is a lake and not linked to the sea. If you want to get to Zurich, the most popular modes of transportation are via plane, rail, or road, as previously described.

Best Time To Visit Zurich

The summer months, from June through August, are ideal for visiting Zurich. This is the most pleasant time of year, with typical temperatures ranging from 18 to 25 degrees Celsius. The city is also less busy this season, since many inhabitants spend their summer vacations in the mountains.

Summer is the best season to visit Zurich if you want to enjoy the outdoors. Swim on Lake Zurich, climb in the neighboring hills, or enjoy a riverboat ride. During the summer, the city also hosts a number of festivals and events, such as the Street Parade and the Zurich Film Festival.

If you're on a tight budget, come during the shoulder seasons of spring (April to May) and fall (September to October). During these months, the weather is still beautiful, and you'll likely find cheaper hotel costs and less tourists.

What To do in Zurich (Top Tourist Activities)

Here are some of the greatest Zurich activities:

- Explore the Old Town: The Grossmünster church, the Rathaus (town hall), and the Kunsthaus Zürich (art gallery) are all located in

Zurich's Old Town, which is a UNESCO World Heritage Site.

- Take a stroll along the Limmat River, which flows through the center of Zurich and is popular for walking, bicycling, and boating. Along the riverfront, there are also a lot of restaurants and cafés, making it a terrific area to people-watch.

- Visit the Kunsthaus Zürich: The Kunsthaus Zürich is one of Switzerland's most prominent art museums, with a collection of over 40,000 pieces of art ranging from the Middle Ages to the present day.

- Shopping on Bahnhofstrasse: Bahnhofstrasse is one of the world's most renowned shopping lanes, including a variety of luxury shops and department stores.

- Take a boat ride on Lake Zurich: this lake is renowned for swimming, boating, and fishing.

There are also boat cruises offered, which are a terrific opportunity to explore the city from a new angle.

- Hike in the Swiss Alps: Zurich is bordered by the Swiss Alps, which provide a range of hiking paths for people of all skill levels.

- Visit a chocolate shop: Switzerland is famous for its chocolate, and Zurich has many chocolate shops where you may try the local delights.

- Enjoy some fondue: Fondue is a typical Swiss delicacy made of melted cheese, and there are many fondue restaurants in Zurich where you can sample this delectable cuisine.

These are just a handful of the numerous activities available in Zurich. Zurich is a city that offers something for everyone, with its rich history, gorgeous environment, and active culture.

Explore Zurich (Top Attractions)

Here are some of Zurich's greatest attractions:

1: The historic core of Zurich, the Old Town, is home to several of the city's most prominent tourist attractions, including the Grossmünster church, the Fraumünster church, and the Rathaus (town hall).

2: Lake Zurich: Lake Zurich is a popular bathing, boating, and fishing destination. Along the lakeshore, there are also various restaurants and cafés.

3: Uetliberg is a mountain that overlooks Zurich. A cable car brings you to the summit, where you can enjoy breathtaking views of the city and surrounding region.

4: Kunsthaus Zurich: The Kunsthaus Zurich is a modern and contemporary art museum. It has nearly 40,000 pieces of art, including paintings, sculptures, and sketches.

5: The Swiss National Museum is a museum dedicated to Swiss history and culture. It has nearly 800,000 pieces in its collection, including archaeological findings, paintings, and sculptures.

6: Zürich Zoo: The Zürich Zoo is one of the world's oldest zoos. It is home to around 4,000 animals from over 300 different species.

These are just a handful of the numerous attractions available in Zurich. Zurich is a city that offers something for everyone, with its rich history, gorgeous environment, and active culture.

Zurich's Suburbs, Cities, and Municipalities

Zurich, Switzerland's biggest city, is separated into various areas, each with its own distinct character and feel. Here are some of Zurich's most notable neighborhoods, cities, and towns:

Altstadt (Old Town): Altstadt is a lovely area in the center of Zurich, with tiny streets, old buildings, and sights such as Grossmünster and Fraumünster. It has a diverse selection of stores, restaurants, and cultural attractions.

Bahnhofstrasse: Bahnhofstrasse runs from Zurich's main railway station to Lake Zurich and is considered one of the world's most prestigious retail avenues. Luxury shops, department stores, and high-end merchants populate the street.

Kreis 4 (Langstrasse): Kreis 4 is a bustling and varied area noted for its nightlife, cosmopolitan environment, and street art. It has a wide selection of fashionable pubs, clubs, and foreign cuisine.

Seefeld: Seefeld is a lovely area on the beaches of Lake Zurich with a peaceful and affluent environment. Beautiful parks, exquisite homes, boutique stores, and waterfront restaurants may be found here.

Zurich West: Previously an industrial district, Zurich West has been significantly redeveloped and is now a hip neighborhood with a creative and contemporary spirit. It is the location of the fashionable Im Viadukt retail complex, as well as art galleries, theaters, and chic pubs.

Wiedikon: Located just south of the city center, Wiedikon is a residential neighborhood with a mix of historic and modern structures. It has a broad selection of stores, restaurants, and cafés, as well as a bustling community vibe.

Oerlikon: Located on Zurich's northern outskirts, Oerlikon is a bustling area recognized for its good transportation and corporate hubs. It has a mix of residential and business neighborhoods, as well as retail complexes and cultural institutions.

Top Tourist Cities to Stay in Zurich

Zurich, Switzerland, is a dynamic and attractive city recognized for its breathtaking natural surroundings, rich history, and high standard of living. If you're planning a trip to Zurich and want to stay in one of the best tourist cities in the area, here are some great options:

Lucerne: A gorgeous city located on the banks of Lake Lucerne, Lucerne is less than an hour's rail trip from Zurich. It's famous for its well-preserved medieval architecture, the landmark Chapel Bridge, and the breathtaking mountain vistas. Don't miss out on a trip to neighboring Mount Pilatus or Mount Rigi.

Interlaken: Interlaken, located between Lake Thun and Lake Brienz, is a famous location for outdoor enthusiasts. It is a gateway to the Bernese Oberland area, which is famous for its spectacular alpine peaks like as the Jungfrau, Eiger, and Mönch. In this adventure paradise, you may go hiking, paragliding, or skiing.

Zermatt: If you like skiing or stunning alpine landscapes, Zermatt is a must-see place. It is well-known for the Matterhorn, one of the world's most recognizable mountains. Explore the beautiful village's car-free streets while skiing, snowboarding, or hiking in the nearby mountains.

Basel is a cultural center recognized for its museums, architecture, and active arts scene. It is located on the border of Switzerland, Germany, and France. Visit the Fondation Beyeler, tour the old town, and if you're lucky, catch the legendary Basel Carnival.

Bern: As Switzerland's capital city, Bern combines history and modernity. Its well-preserved medieval old town, designated as a UNESCO World Heritage Site, is a joy to explore. Bear Park, the Federal Palace, and the Zytglogge clock tower are all must-sees.

These cities are readily accessible from Zurich by rail or vehicle and offer a variety of experiences. Each has its own distinct charm and attractions, making them excellent alternatives for a memorable stay in Zurich.

How long should I Stay in Zurich

The length of a tourist visit in Zurich might vary based on personal tastes, available time, and the particular sites and activities desired. However, the average length of a tourist stay in Zurich is 2 to 3 days. This time period enables tourists to see the city's key attractions, immerse themselves in its cultural offers, and relax in its gorgeous surroundings.

During your stay, you may explore prominent sights such as the Old Town (Altstadt), Lake Zurich, Bahnhofstrasse (one of the world's most exclusive retail avenues), and the city's gorgeous cathedrals and museums. Furthermore, Zurich has a thriving food scene, so you may wish to indulge in Swiss cuisine and sample some local specialties.

If you have more time, try taking day excursions from Zurich to neighboring attractions such as Lucerne, the Rhine Falls, or the picturesque Swiss Alps. These trips will allow you to experience the natural beauty and charm of Switzerland.

Finally, the length of your stay in Zurich is determined by your tastes and the scope of your exploring plans. Whether you have a few days or a few weeks, Zurich has a variety of sights and experiences to suit a variety of interests and make your stay unforgettable.

What to Pack

When visiting Zurich, Switzerland, it is essential to prepare correctly for the weather and activities you want to participate in. Here's a list of things to think about packing for your vacation to Zurich:

Clothing:

Comfy walking shoes: Because Zurich is a pedestrian-friendly city, bring comfy shoes with you.

Weather-appropriate clothing: Before your journey, check the weather prediction to prepare properly. Because Zurich has a mild temperature, carry a combination of lightweight and warmer clothing layers. Even in the summer, nights may be chilly, so a lightweight jacket or sweater is necessary.

Pack a small umbrella or a waterproof jacket since rain showers might occur throughout the year in Zurich.

Travel Necessities:

Passport and travel papers: Make sure you have a valid passport as well as any required visas or travel documents.

carry a travel adapter: Switzerland utilizes the Type J plug, so carry one with you to charge your electrical gadgets.

Bring some Swiss Francs or a travel card to ensure you have local cash for modest purchases.

Travel insurance: Having travel insurance that covers medical emergencies, trip cancellation, and lost possessions is always a smart idea.

Accessories and Electronics:

Smartphone and charger: Stay connected while navigating the city.

Camera: Zurich has stunning landscape, so bring your camera to record the moments.

Keep your gadgets charged while on the move with a power bank.

Adapters and cords: Bring any cables required for your electrical gadgets.

Personal Effects:

Bring travel-sized amenities such as a toothbrush, toothpaste, shampoo, conditioner, and any other personal care things you may need.

drugs: If you need prescription drugs, make sure you bring enough for the length of your vacation.

Personal hygiene items: Bring soap, deodorant, and any other goods you choose to use.

Remember to pack light and keep the length of your vacation in mind. It's also a good idea to double-check the airline's luggage policies to prevent any surprises at the airport.

Zurich Visa Tips

Switzerland, which includes Zurich, is a member of the Schengen Area. Citizens of some countries, including Switzerland, are permitted to enter the Schengen Area without a visa for short periods. The particular regulations for visa exemption may differ based on your nationality.

Who Needs a Visa to Enter Zurich?

Citizens of the following countries may generally visit Switzerland and remain for up to 90 days during a 180-day period without requiring a visa:

Members of the European Union (EU) and the European Free Trade Association (EFTA) have the right to enter and remain in Switzerland without a visa.
Citizens of the United States, Canada, Australia, New Zealand, and Japan may visit Switzerland without a visa for up to 90 days during a 180-day period for tourism or business.

Several additional countries: Switzerland has visa waiver arrangements with a number of foreign countries. To confirm visa requirements, consult the official website of Switzerland's Federal Department of Foreign Affairs or contact the Swiss embassy or consulate in your home country.

Zurich Visa Application

You will normally need to provide the following papers when applying for a Schengen visa:

- Form for visa application completed.
- Valid passport with at least six months validity beyond the duration of your planned stay.
- Two passport-sized photos taken recently.
- Proof of travel medical insurance with at least 30,000 Euros in coverage.
- Flight itinerary or evidence of transportation arrangements.
- Hotel bookings or an invitation letter from a host are examples of proof of accommodation in Zurich.

- Proof that you have enough money to cover your stay in Switzerland.
- Itinerary or comprehensive plan of your Zurich activities.
- Employment letters, property ownership, or family links are examples of proof of ties to your native country.

It should be noted that visa requirements differ based on your nationality and the purpose of your travel.

Must-See Landmarks & Monuments in Zurich

Zurich, Switzerland's biggest city, is noted for its gorgeous architecture, rich history, and attractive scenery. Here are some of Zurich's must-see sights and monuments:

Fraumünster: Another magnificent church, the Fraumünster is well-known for its spectacular stained glass windows designed by renowned artist Marc

Chagall. The church has a long history that dates back to the 9th century.

Bahnhofstrasse: This world-famous retail route connects Zurich Central Station to Lake Zurich. It's a hive of luxury shops, department stores, and cafés, making it ideal for a leisurely walk.

Lake Zurich: While not a monument or landmark in and of itself, Lake Zurich contributes significantly to the city's attractiveness. Enjoy the gorgeous surroundings by taking a boat trip, swimming, or just relaxing on the lake's beach.

Zurich Opera House: As one of Europe's major opera houses, the Zurich Opera House is a must-see for art and music lovers. Attend a concert or take a guided tour to appreciate its magnificent architecture and interior.

Kunsthaus Zurich: This famous art museum has a large collection of modern and contemporary art, including works by Swiss painters as well as internationally recognized artists such as Monet, Picasso, and Van Gogh.

Uetliberg: A journey to Uetliberg is strongly recommended for nature enthusiasts. It is Zurich's local mountain, with spectacular views of the city and the Swiss Alps. Hike to the top or take the train for a more leisurely experience.

Swiss National Museum: Located near the major railway station in a stunning old structure, the Swiss National Museum offers an in-depth look at Swiss culture, history, and art. Explore the exhibitions to learn about the country's history.

Zurich Zoo: If you're traveling with children or just like animals, the Zurich Zoo is a must-see. It is home to many different animals, including elephants, lions, penguins, and others. The zoo is also concerned in conservation and education.

These are just a handful of Zurich's numerous outstanding sites and monuments. Each one provides a different viewpoint on the city's history, culture, and natural beauty.

Contemporary Art Galleries and Museums

Zurich has a thriving contemporary art scene, with galleries and institutions displaying works by local and international artists. Here are some important Zurich contemporary art galleries and museums:

Kunsthaus Zurich: One of the city's most prominent art institutions, the Kunsthaus Zurich has a wide collection of modern and contemporary art. It is home to works by well-known painters such as Monet, Picasso, Giacometti, and Warhol.

The Kunsthalle Zurich is a contemporary art facility in Zurich that focuses on exhibiting innovative and experimental art forms. It features exhibits, films, performances, and activities by contemporary artists on a regular basis.

Galerie Eva Presenhuber: Renowned for its excellent roster of contemporary artists, Galerie Eva Presenhuber exhibits a variety of creative activities including painting, sculpture, photography, and installations.

Galerie Gmurzynska focuses on modern and contemporary art, with a specific emphasis on Russian avant-garde and European post-war art. It represents Picasso, Miró, Chagall, and Yves Klein, among others.

Galerie Peter Kilchmann presents contemporary art in a variety of mediums, including painting, sculpture, photography, and video. It represents both developing and renowned Swiss and international artists.

BolteLang is a contemporary art gallery that exhibits unique and experimental works by rising artists. It supports multidisciplinary approaches and organizes shows that push the bounds of conventional aesthetic boundaries.

Mai 36 Galerie: Mai 36 Galerie showcases contemporary art in a variety of genres such as photography, painting, and sculpture. It represents globally renowned artists and works with curators to deliver exciting shows.

These are only a handful of Zurich's greatest modern art galleries and institutions. The city offers a diverse cultural environment, and there are several galleries and exhibition locations to visit.

Zurich National Parks and Reserve

Zurich, Switzerland, is not well-known for its national parks or reserves. However, in and around Zurich, there are various wonderful natural regions and parks where you may enjoy nature and outdoor sports. Here are a few examples:

Zurichberg: Located in Zurich's northern outskirts, Zurichberg is a steep location with a park that provides breathtaking views of the city and surrounding environment. It's a wonderful spot for strolling, picnics, and relaxing in nature.

Lake Zurich: Lake Zurich is a lovely lake that runs along the city's southeastern border. It provides a variety of leisure options, such as swimming, boating, and lakeside walks. Along the lake's shoreline, there are various parks and green areas to relax and enjoy the view, including Seefeld Park and Belvoir Park.

Uetliberg: Uetliberg is a mountain situated just outside of Zurich that offers spectacular views of the city and the Alps. It's a popular hiking and walking path location with a variety of ways to explore. The region is readily accessible by public transit, and the top has a café and a viewing tower.

These regions, although beautiful and offering recreational possibilities, are not formally recognized as national parks or reserves. Switzerland as a whole, on the other hand, includes various national parks and natural reserves, such as the Swiss National Park in the Engadine area, approximately a 3-hour drive from Zurich. If you have the chance to go outside of Zurich, these protected areas provide unique flora, wildlife, and ecosystems that are worth investigating.

Romantic Packs and Gardens for Couples

There are several beautiful couples packs and gardens in Zurich where you may spend precious time with your loved one. Here are a few ideas:

Lindenhof Park: Lindenhof Park, located in Zurich's old center, provides a calm and romantic ambiance. Picnics may be enjoyed on the beautiful green grounds while taking in panoramic views of the city and the Limmat River.

Chinese Garden: This lovely garden is a hidden treasure in Zurich. It is inspired by traditional Chinese gardens and has tranquil ponds, pavilions, and vibrant vegetation. Take a leisurely walk with your lover and absorb in the tranquil atmosphere.

Botanical Garden: The University of Zurich's Botanical Garden is a joy for nature enthusiasts. It has a diverse collection of plants and flowers from all around the globe. Explore the many themed parts with your family and marvel at nature's beauty.

Belvoir Park: Belvoir Park, located on the banks of Lake Zurich, provides a lovely location for couples. The park has beautiful gardens, a beautiful lakefront, and walking routes. Bring a picnic or dine at the park's restaurant for a romantic dinner.

Rieterpark: Located near the Zurich Kunsthaus, this attractive park is noted for its gorgeous scenery and refined ambiance. It has wide lawns, tree-lined walkways, and tiny ponds. Take a romantic stroll or locate a quiet place to rest and unwind.

Sechseläutenplatz: While not technically a garden, Sechseläutenplatz is a large plaza near Lake Zurich. Throughout the year, it holds a variety of events and marketplaces. If you go during the summer, you could catch an open-air concert or festival, which provides a vibrant and lovely ambiance.

Before you go, be sure to verify the opening hours and any access restrictions for these venues. Have a nice weekend together in Zurich!

Festivals & Events in Zurich

Zurich, Switzerland, is a lively city that holds a variety of festivals and events throughout the year. Here are some prominent Zurich festivals and events:

Zurich Street Parade: Zurich Street Parade is one of the world's biggest techno music events. It is held in August and draws hundreds of thousands of music fans who congregate to dance and revel in Zurich's streets.

The Zurich Film Festival is an annual event held in September that showcases a varied variety of foreign films. The festival welcomes world-renowned filmmakers, actors, and industry experts.

Sechseläuten: Sechseläuten is a typical Zurich spring festivity. It takes place on April 3rd and celebrates the conclusion of the winter season. The burning of the "Böögg," a snowman-like creature representing winter, is the festival's climax.

Zurich Christmas Market: With its charming Christmas markets, Zurich turns into a winter paradise throughout the holiday season. The major market is situated in the city center and offers a variety of food, beverages, crafts, and souvenirs.

Zurich event: Taking place in June and July, the Zurich Festival is a multidisciplinary arts event. It presents a broad schedule of music, theater, dance, and visual arts performances, drawing world-renowned performers.

Knabenschiessen is a classic shooting tournament conducted in Zurich every year. It takes place in September and is available to young people aged 13 to 17. The event also features carnival rides, food vendors, and live entertainment.

The Zurich Street Food Festival is a well-known gourmet event that brings together food sellers from diverse cultures. Visitors may try a variety of different delicacies while listening to live music and entertainment.

Zurich Pride Festival: The Zurich Pride Festival takes place every June. It features a colorful procession through the city center, as well as celebrations, cultural activities, and talks advocating equality and honoring variety.

These are just a handful of the festivals and events that occur in Zurich. The city boasts a diverse cultural calendar that offers something for everyone all year.

Zurich's Luxury Tourist Hotels & Resorts

Here are some of the most luxurious hotels in Zurich, along with their prices:

Baur au Lac - Located in the center of Zurich, this hotel provides beautiful views of the city. It has a Michelin-starred restaurant, a spa, and a lovely garden. Rates begin at $1,000 per night.

The Dolder Grand - Located on a hill above Zurich, this hotel provides breathtaking views of the city and the Alps. There is a Michelin-starred restaurant, a spa, and a golf course on the premises. Rates begin at $1,500 per night.

Storchen - This hotel in Zurich's Old Town provides a unique and historic experience. It boasts a Michelin-starred restaurant, a bar, and a rooftop patio with city views. Rates begin at $800 per night.

Widder Hotel - Located in Zurich's Old Town, this hotel provides a contemporary and trendy experience. It features a restaurant, a bar, and a spa. Rates begin at $700 per night.

Park Hyatt Zurich - Located in the centre of Zurich, this hotel provides a magnificent and contemporary experience. There is a spa, a fitness facility, and many eateries. Rates begin at $900 per night.

These are just a handful of Zurich's numerous luxury hotels. With so many alternatives, you're certain to discover the ideal hotel for your preferences and budget.

Budget Friendly Hotels and Resorts

Here are some reasonably priced hotels and resorts in Zurich:

Ruby Mimi Hotel Zurich: Located in the center of Zurich, this hotel provides contemporary rooms with complimentary WiFi. Prices begin at CHF 100 per night.

Ruby Mimi Hotel Zurich Hotel Kindli: Located in the Old Town, this hotel provides classic rooms with complimentary WiFi. Prices begin at CHF 120 per night.

MEININGER Hotel Zürich Greencity: Located in Zurich's West area, this hostel provides contemporary dorms and private rooms with free WiFi. Prices begin at CHF 40 per night.

CitizenM Zürich: Located in the Old Town, this hotel provides trendy rooms with complimentary WiFi and a 24-hour bar. Prices begin at CHF 150 per night.

Acasa Suites: Located in Zurich Nord, this apartment hotel provides contemporary units with free WiFi and a kitchenette. Prices begin at CHF 180 per night.

These are just a handful of Zurich's numerous budget-friendly hotels and resorts. You can locate a terrific location to stay that meets your budget and requirements with a little investigation.

Tourist Apartments and Vacation Rentals in Zurich

Here are some of the nicest apartments and holiday rentals in Zurich, as well as their prices:

1: Studio Gocki is a studio apartment in Zurich's Old Town. It has a kitchenette, a bathroom, and a television. The nightly rate is $120.

2: The apartment Le Bijou Bahnhofstrasse / Paradeplatz ist in Zürich, zwischen der Bahnhofstrasse und dem Paradeplatz. It is furnished with two bedrooms, a kitchen, a living room, and a balcony. The fee each night is $200.

3: Löwenplatz Apartment between Station by Airhome is an apartment in Zurich's Old Town, between the Löwenplatz and the railway station. It is furnished with two bedrooms, a kitchen, a living room, and a balcony. The nightly rate is $180.

These are just a handful of the many fantastic Zurich flats and holiday rentals. The cost of living will vary based on the size of the flat, its location, and the season.

Here are some pointers for discovering cheap Zurich apartments and holiday rentals:

1: Plan ahead of time, particularly if you're going during high season.

2: Consider staying somewhere less central. Suburban apartments and holiday rentals are often less expensive than those in the city center.

3: Look for apartments and vacation homes that provide discounts for longer stays.

4: Consider renting out an apartment or a vacation home to friends or relatives. This may assist to lower the cost of lodging.
I hope this was helpful!

Zurich Tourist Guesthouses and Hostels

Here are some of the most affordable tourist guesthouses and hostels in Zurich, Switzerland:

1: The Zurich Youth Hostel is a popular budget option, with dorm beds beginning at CHF 30 per night. It is centrally positioned in the city, near to all important attractions.

2: A more contemporary choice is the Green Marmot Capsule Hotel Zürich, where capsule beds start at CHF 40 per night. It's also at a fantastic position, only steps away from the railway station.

3: Study2Night City Center Hostel is another affordable choice, with dorm beds beginning at CHF 35 per night. It's in a peaceful neighborhood, only a short walk from the city center.

4: Study2Night City Center Hostel in Zurich is a warm and communal hostel with dorm beds beginning at

CHF 35 per night. It is in a fantastic position, near to many of the main attractions.

5: Viktoria Budget Hostel is a clean and pleasant hostel that offers dorm beds for as little as CHF 30 per night. It's in a peaceful neighborhood, only a short walk from the city center.

6: For those seeking a more traditional hostel experience, Oldtown Hostel Otter is an excellent choice. Dorm beds cost from CHF 35 per night. It is centrally positioned in the Old Town, near to many important attractions.

These are just a handful of Zurich's numerous excellent tourist guesthouses and hostels. With so many possibilities, you're sure to discover the ideal location to stay for your budget and requirements.

Zurich Tourist Camp Locations and Prices

Here are some of the best-rated tourist camps in Zurich, Switzerland, along with their prices:

Camping Fischers Fritz: Located on the beaches of Lake Zurich, this campground provides a range of accommodation choices, including tents, caravans, and RVs. There is also a restaurant, a bar, and a swimming pool. Prices for a tent spot start at CHF 30 per night.

Camping in Atzmännig: Located in the picturesque Atzmännig mountains, this campground provides spectacular views of the surrounding region. It offers a range of lodging alternatives, including as tents, cabins, and chalets. Prices for a tent spot start at CHF 40 per night.

Camping on Lützelau Island: This campground provides a one-of-a-kind camping experience on a tiny island in the center of Lake Zurich. It only has a few pitches and is only accessible by boat. Prices for a tent spot start at CHF 50 per night.

Camping at the Strandbad Stampf: Located on the banks of Lake Zurich, this campground is famous for swimming and sunbathing. Tents, caravans, and RVs are among the available accommodations. For a tent spot, prices start at CHF 25 per night.

Lake Walen Camping: This campground is situated on the shores of Lake Walen and provides breathtaking views of the surrounding mountains. Tents, caravans, and RVs are among the available accommodations. Prices for a tent spot start at CHF 35 per night.

Please keep in mind that these are only a handful of the numerous tourist camp locations in Zurich. Prices may vary based on the season and the kind of accommodation selected.

Nightlife in Zurich

Zurich's nightlife is a sensory overload. There's something for everyone, from the thriving music scene to the delectable cuisine and beverages. You'll have a terrific time whether you want to dance the night away or just relax with pals. And, with its breathtaking vistas of the Alps, Zurich is the ideal setting for a night out.

It's a great opportunity to learn about the city's culture and diversity. There's something for everyone among its many pubs, clubs, and events. So, whether you're a native or a guest, don't miss out on Zurich's nightlife scene.

Tips for Having a Wonderful Night in Zurich

Here are some pointers for having a memorable night out:

Do your homework: Before you head out, do some research on the various nightlife alternatives in your neighborhood. This will allow you to narrow down your options and pick the ideal location for your mood and budget.

Make an effort to look your best: First impressions are important, so dress to impress when you go out. This does not imply that you must wear a suit or gown, but you should make an attempt to seem presentable.

Go with a group of buddies: Going out with pals is usually more enjoyable than going out by yourself. You'll not only have someone to speak to, but you'll also have someone looking out for you.

Don't be frightened to get up and dance: Dancing is an excellent way to relax and have fun. If you don't know how to dance, just move your body to the music. You'll be astonished at how much enjoyment you get out of it.

Don't overdo it with alcohol: When you're out partying, it's tempting to get caught up in the moment and overindulge. However, it is important to pace yourself and drink wisely.

<u>Keep an eye on your surroundings</u>: When you're out at night, it's critical to be alert of your surroundings. This entails being cautious of your own space and alert to any hazards.

Have a good time! The most essential thing is to enjoy yourself and have fun. So unwind, let go, and dance the night away.

<u>Here are few more tips</u>

If you don't know where to go, ask your friends or family for suggestions.

- Before you travel, read internet evaluations of various places.

- Make sure you have a proper ID if you're heading to a club.
- To prevent lengthy queues, arrive early.

- Take a break and go for a stroll outdoors if you're feeling fatigued.

- Remember to stay hydrated! Before, during, and after your night out, drink lots of water.

- Use a designated driver or a cab to go home.

Following these guidelines can help you have a safe and fun night out.

Zurich's Active Nightclubs and Bars

Here are a few well-known Zurich establishments:

Hive Club: Hive Club, located in Zurich's industrial sector, is a famous club noted for its electronic music and energetic atmosphere. It provides a wide range of events such as DJ sets, live concerts, and themed parties.

Mascotte: Mascotte is a historic nightclub in the centre of Zurich that has been entertaining visitors since the

1920s. It caters to a varied population by combining live music, DJ performances, and themed events.

Kaufleuten: This well-known facility is set in a historic guild house and comprises a nightclub, bar, and restaurant. Kaufleuten presents a diverse variety of events, from worldwide DJ club nights to live concerts and cultural acts.

Plaza Klub: Plaza Klub, located near Zurich's major railway station, is renowned for its lively club nights and live music events. It has a large dance floor and plays a range of genres such as electronic, hip-hop, and house music.

Longstreet Bar: Longstreet Bar, located in Zurich's Old Town, is a popular location with a dynamic atmosphere. It serves a wide range of beverages and often has live music performances ranging from jazz and blues to rock and pop.

Remember to double-check each venue's schedule, admission regulations, and age limits, since they may differ based on the event and day of the week.

Where to Go for Live Music and Jazz in Zurich

In Zurich, there are several options for finding live music and jazz places. Here are a few recommendations:

Examine the websites of nearby music venues: Many venues maintain webpages that list forthcoming performances. To be alerted of new events, you may also sign up for email newsletters.

Make use of a live music guide online: A lot of websites provide listings of live music events in Zurich. Some of these websites also enable you to narrow down your search results by genre, date, and location.

Consult with your friends and relatives: If you have any Zurich contacts, they may be able to suggest some nice live music places.

Take a stroll across the city: Many of Zurich's live music venues may be found in the Old Town and Zurich West. Take a trip around these places and see what you can locate if you're not sure where to begin.

Zurich Jazz and Live Music Venues

There are various locations in Zurich that provide live music and jazz events.
Here are some of Zurich's greatest live music and jazz venues:

Moods: Moods is a well-known jazz club in the Schiffbau building. Throughout the year, it features a range of jazz, soul, and world music performances. The venue offers a terrific ambience and a committed jazz audience.

JazzNoJazz Festival: The JazzNoJazz Festival is an annual event hosted in Zurich that features an international jazz artist lineup. The event is held at several locations across the city and features a wide variety of jazz genres.

Jazz Club Mampf: Jazz Club Mampf is a charming venue that provides live jazz concerts on a regular basis. It is located in the centre of Zurich and provides an intimate atmosphere for appreciating jazz music. It often features local talent.

Kaufleuten is a prominent Zurich venue that offers a range of events, including live music performances. While it is not strictly a jazz venue, jazz performers and bands, as well as other genres, are periodically featured.

Mehrspur is a cultural facility housed in the historic Kinski building. It provides a venue for a variety of musical genres, including jazz. You may hear live jazz concerts as well as other types of music here.

Exil: Exil is a bustling Zurich club that hosts live music performances of many genres, including jazz. It has a lively environment and often hosts both local and international jazz performers.

Theater Rigiblick is a theater and cultural institution recognized for its varied programming, which includes jazz performances. It offers a one-of-a-kind venue for live jazz concerts in Zurich.

These venues cater to a variety of preferences by providing a variety of live music experiences, including jazz.

Zurich Food and Cuisines

Zurich's culinary tapestry weaves flavors that thrill both inhabitants and visitors, resulting in a dynamic blend of cultures and tastes. The city's cuisine culture tantalizes the senses with its exquisite range, ranging from hearty Swiss staples like fondue and rösti to inventive gourmet inventions. Every mouthful in Zurich is a trip, where traditions meet innovation and residents and visitors alike relish the symphony of tastes that make this city a genuine gastronomic marvel.

Zurich Favorite Food and Cuisine

Zurich, Switzerland's biggest city, has a broad selection of gastronomic pleasures that are appreciated by both residents and visitors. Here are some Zurich residents' favorite dishes and cuisines:

- Swiss food is highly valued in Zurich, and inhabitants take pleasure in their traditional meals. Fondue and raclette are classic cheese-based delicacies that should not be missed. Another popular Swiss food is rösti, which is prepared from grated and fried potatoes.

- Chocolate: Zurich, like the rest of Switzerland, is known for its high-quality chocolate. There are several chocolatiers and chocolate businesses selling delightful delights. Zurich's well-known chocolate brands include Lindt, Sprüngli, and Teuscher.

- Zürcher Geschnetzeltes: A Zurich delicacy composed of sliced veal stewed in a creamy white wine and mushroom sauce. It is popular among both residents and tourists, and is often served with Rösti or noodles.

- foreign Cuisine: Zurich has a thriving culinary scene with a diverse selection of foreign cuisines. Throughout the city, there are outstanding Italian, French, Mediterranean, Asian, and Middle Eastern restaurants. There are alternatives for every taste, from traditional pizza and spaghetti to sushi, falafel, and curries.

- Street Food: Zurich's street food culture has risen in prominence, with several food trucks and kiosks selling delectable and unique meals. Street food in Zurich provides a wide and delectable experience, ranging from gourmet burgers and hot dogs to Middle Eastern wraps and Asian fusion cuisine.

- Bakeries and Pastries: Fresh bread, pastries, and sweet delights are popular in Swiss bakeries. Zurich has several bakeries where you can get freshly made croissants, pretzels, tarts, and Swiss delicacies like Nusstorte (nut tart) and Mandelbiber (almond gingerbread).

- Farmers' Markets: Visiting Zurich's farmers' markets is a terrific opportunity to learn about local food and culinary delicacies. Fresh fruits and vegetables, cheeses, meats, and other regional items are available. It's a fantastic chance to try local cuisine and take in the lively environment.

These are just a handful of the beloved dishes and cuisines enjoyed by Zurich residents and visitors alike. The city has a diverse gastronomic scene with something to suit every taste.

Vegetarian and Vegan Restaurants in Zurich

Zurich, Switzerland's biggest city, has a wide range of vegetarian and vegan culinary alternatives. Here are some restaurants in Zurich where you may enjoy vegetarian and vegan food:

Hiltl: Founded in 1898, Hiltl is the world's oldest vegetarian restaurant. It serves a large variety of vegetarian and vegan cuisine, as well as a buffet with over 100 selections. They also have a Hiltl Shop that sells vegan goods.

Tibits: Tibits is a popular vegetarian and vegan buffet-style restaurant. Soups, salads, hot meals, and desserts are among the many fresh and seasonal items available.

Vegan Kitchen is a vegan fast-food restaurant that serves a wide range of plant-based burgers, wraps, sandwiches, and salads. Vegan sweets and smoothies are also available.

Beetnut is a vegan restaurant that specializes in healthful, plant-based meals. Salads, bowls, and burgers cooked from fresh and organic ingredients are available.

Roots and Friends: Roots and Friends is a vegetarian restaurant with an international cuisine menu. They provide vegetarian and vegan alternatives such as burgers, bowls, and desserts.

The Sacred is a vegan café and bakery that provides plant-based breakfast and lunch. They also have vegan pastries and sweets available.

Vegelateria: Vegelateria is a vegan ice cream store that serves dairy-free ice cream produced from plant-based components. There are also gluten-free and soy-free choices available.

These are just a handful of Zurich's numerous vegetarian and vegan-friendly restaurants and cafés. There is a booming plant-based cuisine culture in the city, so you will have lots of alternatives.

Best Cafes & Restaurants in Zurich

Zurich, Switzerland's biggest city, has a thriving culinary scene with a diverse selection of cafés and restaurants. Here are some of the greatest restaurants and bars in Zurich:

Kronenhalle: Kronenhalle is a historical Zurich institution recognized for its traditional Swiss food and exquisite ambience. Since its inception in 1924, the restaurant has been a favorite of artists, politicians, and townspeople.

Zeughauskeller: Located in a historic structure, Zeughauskeller is well-known for its classic Swiss fare, such as substantial sausages and roasted meats. The comfortable environment and large beer variety make it a favorite among both residents and visitors.

Frau Gerolds Garten: Frau Gerolds Garten, located in Zurich's fashionable West area, is a one-of-a-kind mix of a restaurant, bar, and urban garden. While surrounded by nature and art installations, enjoy a peaceful ambiance, excellent cuisine, and cool beverages.

Clouds: Clouds, located on the 35th story of the Prime Tower, provides stunning panoramic views of Zurich as well as sophisticated European cuisine. You'll have a memorable dining experience whether you come for lunch, dinner, or drinks.

Maison Manesse: This Michelin-starred Zurich restaurant employs fresh and locally sourced ingredients to produce unique and artistically presented meals. The tasting meal highlights the chef's ingenuity and culinary abilities.

Schwarzenbach Kolonialwaren is more than simply a café; it is a coffee and tea merchant with a long history. Step inside this quaint, traditional shop and treat yourself to a cup of well prepared coffee or tea and a piece of baked cake.

La Stanza: If you're craving Italian food, go to La Stanza. This family-run restaurant provides traditional Italian fare such as handmade pasta and wood-fired pizza. It is a popular option because of its warm environment and polite service.

These are just a handful of Zurich's many amazing cafés and eateries. Zurich provides something for everyone's taste, whether it's classic Swiss dining, foreign cuisine, or contemporary places.

Dining Etiquette in Zurich

Here are some Zurich eating etiquette tips:

- Put on proper clothing. Because Zurich is a global city, you may dress casually at most restaurants. If you're going to a fine-dining institution, though, you should dress up a little.

- Be punctual. Because Swiss people are notoriously punctual, it is essential that you arrive on time for your reservation. If you're going to be late, phone the restaurant ahead of time to let them know.

- Be courteous to the personnel. Because Swiss people are recognized for their politeness, it is essential to be kind to the restaurant employees. You should address them as "Herr" or "Frau" followed by their surname.

- Before you begin eating, make sure everyone is seated. It is considered impolite to begin eating before everyone at the table has taken their seats.

- Make use of your napkin. Place your napkin on your lap when you sit. After eating, use it to clean your lips.
- You should not speak with your mouth full. It is considered impolite to speak with your mouth full.

- Slurp your soup instead. Slurping your soup is also considered impolite.

- Don't leave anything on your plate. It's considered impolite to leave food on your plate, particularly if you're a visitor.

- Order the least priced item on the menu. It is considered impolite to order the most costly item on the menu, particularly while visiting someone's house.

- Smoking is not permitted in restaurants. Smoking is not permitted in Zurich restaurants.

- Please tip your server. Tipping your waiter 10-15% of the amount is usual.

  - ☐ *Here are few more Zurich eating recommendations:*

- If you are unsure what to order, ask your waitress for suggestions. They would gladly assist you in selecting something you will appreciate.

- If you're on a tight budget, Zurich has lots of inexpensive eateries. There are also numerous eateries that provide lunch specials.

- Try one of Zurich's numerous ethnic restaurants for a one-of-a-kind eating experience. Japanese, Thai, and Indian cuisine are all available.

- Don't forget to sample some of the local delicacies. Zurich is known for a variety of delectable foods, including fondue, raclette, and Zürcher Geschnetzeltes.

I hope these suggestions help you have a memorable eating experience in Zurich.

Zurich Currency

The Swiss Franc (CHF) is the currency of Zurich, Switzerland. The following are the most popular denominations of Swiss Franc banknotes and coins:
Banknotes: 10 CHF, 20 CHF, 50 CHF, 100 CHF, 200 CHF, and 1,000 CHF

10 rappen (0.10 CHF), 20 rappen (0.20 CHF), 12 franc (0.50 CHF), 1 franc (1 CHF), 2 francs (2 CHF), 5 francs (5 CHF), 10 francs (10 CHF)

These denominations span a wide range of values, making it possible to conduct transactions in Zurich and across Switzerland. It should be noted that the 1 rappen (0.01 CHF) coin is no longer in circulation and is seldom used.

Switzerland is well-known for its high-quality banknotes with advanced security mechanisms to prevent counterfeiting.

Where Can I Exchange Money?

There are various money exchange locations in Zurich. Here are several possibilities:

Banks: The majority of Zurich's main banks provide currency exchange services. UBS, Credit Suisse, and Zürcher Kantonalbank are three of the city's well-known institutions where you may exchange money. Inquire about their exchange rates and costs at their branches.

Currency Exchange Offices: Currency exchange offices are situated across Zurich. These businesses specialize in foreign exchange and provide competitive prices. Change Migros, Travelex, and Euro Change are among well-known exchange offices in Zurich.

Currency exchange counters may be found at Zurich Airport and major railway stations such as Zurich Hauptbahnhof if you arrive in Zurich by air or train. Keep in mind that exchange rates at airports and railway stations may be lower than in the city core.

Post Offices: Swiss post offices provide currency exchange services as well. Look for signs that say "PostFinance" or "Post" and inquire about their exchange rates and costs.

Hotels: Some Zurich hotels provide currency exchange services to their visitors. However, to guarantee you're obtaining a reasonable exchange rate, check their prices with other providers.

When converting money, it's important to check rates and fees at several sites to obtain the best bargain. Also, be prepared to provide your identity papers in accordance with local legislation.

LGBTQ + Acceptance

Zurich is a very welcoming city for LGBTQ+ persons. Since 2022, same-sex marriage has been legal in Switzerland, and there are several services and organizations available to help LGBTQ+ persons.

Here are some crucial elements about LGBTQ+ acceptance in Zurich:

Legal Protections: Switzerland allowed same-sex sexual conduct in 1942, and sexual orientation discrimination has been illegal under federal law since 1995. The Swiss parliament enacted the "Marriage for All" bill in 2021, allowing same-sex marriage across the country, including in Zurich.

LGBTQ+ groups: Zurich is home to a number of LGBTQ+ groups that seek to promote acceptance, provide assistance, and advocate for the community's rights. The Zurich Pride Festival, which arranges activities and festivities every year, and Pink Cross, a national LGBTQ+ group established in Zurich, are two examples.

Zurich has a thriving LGBTQ+ culture, with various LGBTQ+-friendly institutions such as pubs, clubs, and cafés. Kreis 4 and Kreis 5 are well-known for their LGBTQ+-friendly clubs and activities.

Healthcare and assistance: Zurich provides health care and assistance to LGBTQ+ people. There are specialist healthcare providers that cater to the LGBTQ+ community's needs, such as clinics that provide gender-affirming therapies and mental health services.

Anti-Discrimination Laws: Zurich has anti-discrimination legislation in effect to protect persons from discrimination based on sexual orientation and gender identity in a variety of settings, including work, housing, and public accommodations. These laws attempt to provide LGBTQ+ people with equal treatment and opportunity.

LGBTQ+ Awareness and Education: Through different projects, Zurich promotes LGBTQ+ awareness and education. Zurich schools teach on LGBTQ+ problems, and there are educational initiatives and seminars to encourage tolerance and acceptance.

While Zurich has achieved great progress, it is crucial to recognize that problems and discrimination against LGBTQ+ people still persist. However, Zurich's general attitude toward LGBTQ+ acceptance is favorable, and the city is working hard to create an open and friendly atmosphere for all of its people.

Zurich Emergency Contacts

The following are Zurich's most significant emergency contacts:

117 police officers
118th Fire Department
144 Medical Emergencies
Mountain rescue number: 1414
144 ambulances
Poison control number: 145
0800 800 700 for roadside help.
044 255 11 11 for lost and found 044 251 51 51 for tourist information
In an emergency, dial 112, which is the European emergency number. Calls to 112 are free from any landline, payphone, or cell phone.

Cultural Etiquette and Customs in Zurich

Zurich, Switzerland's biggest city, has its own cultural etiquettes that tourists should be aware of. Here are some important things to remember about cultural etiquette in Zurich:

- Punctuality is highly valued in Switzerland, thus being on time for appointments, meetings, or social occasions is essential. Even being a few minutes late may be considered rude.

- Greetings: When meeting someone for the first time, the most popular form of greeting in Zurich is a handshake. Maintain eye contact and say "Guten Morgen" (Good morning), "Guten Tag" (Good day), or "Guten Abend" (Good evening) depending on the time of day.

- Personal Space: Swiss people often value their personal space, so keep a respectable distance while chatting with others. Touching or embracing someone you've just met may be considered invasive unless done in a social setting.

- Quietness is valued among Zurich locals, and noisy or disruptive conduct is typically frowned upon, particularly in public areas, restaurants, and public transportation. Maintain a quiet voice and avoid making unneeded noise.

- Tipping: In Zurich, service costs are often included in restaurant and hotel bills. However, as a token of gratitude for excellent service, it is traditional to round up the amount or offer a little tip (typically 5-10%). You may also tip taxi drivers and hotel employees if you believe they offered excellent service.

- Dress Code: Zurich is a fashion-conscious city where people dress cleanly and modestly. It is best to dress modestly while visiting churches, with shoulders and knees covered.

- Recycling and cleanliness: Switzerland is well-known for its environmental stewardship and cleanliness. Zurich has a good recycling system, so be sure to sort your trash properly.

Furthermore, public places are highly appreciated, so prevent littering and dispose of rubbish in appropriate containers.

- Respect for Privacy: Swiss people appreciate their privacy, therefore be polite and refrain from inquiring about personal concerns except in the context of a strong connection or friendship.

By following these cultural etiquettes, you may demonstrate respect for Zurich's local traditions and enrich your visit to the city.

Top Money Saving Strategies

If you're a first-time tourist to Zurich and want to save money, try the following strategies:

- Plan your vacation for the off-season: Zurich may be pricey, particularly during the high tourist season. Consider going during the shoulder seasons (spring or fall), when the weather is still beautiful but lodging and attraction costs are often reduced.

- Look for low-cost rooms: Zurich has a wide selection of accommodations, from luxury hotels to low-cost ones. Find low-cost hotels, guesthouses, or hostels that meet your budget. Consider lodging just outside of the city center, where costs are often cheaper.

- Use public transportation: Zurich's public transit system is efficient and well-connected. To save money on transit, get a Zurich Card or a day pass. It allows you to unrestricted travel throughout the city on trams, buses, trains, and even boats.

- Explore free attractions: Zurich offers a variety of free attractions and activities. Take a walk around Lake Zurich, see the ancient town (Altstadt), visit cathedrals such as Grossmünster und Fraumünster, or relax in the parks and gardens.

- Pack your own snacks: Because eating out in Zurich may be pricey, try bringing your own snacks or having a picnic in one of the parks. To get cheap food and beverages, visit the city's grocery shops or local markets.

- Use tap water: Because Switzerland's tap water is of high quality, there is no need to purchase bottled water. Bring a reusable water bottle that you may refill anytime you need to remain hydrated.

- Use free museum days: Many museums in Zurich provide free entry on certain days or seasons of the year. To save money on admission prices, research the museums you're interested in and organize your visit appropriately.

- Look for specials and discounts: Look for deals, discounts, or city passes that may save you money on attractions, restaurants, or transportation. Special discounts are often available on websites such as Groupon or the official Zurich Tourism website.

- Zurich is a walkable city, and visiting it on foot may be a terrific way to save money while enjoying its beauty. You may also use the city's bike-sharing program to hire a bike, which is a cost-effective and environmentally responsible way to move about.

- Avoid excessive foreign conversion costs by checking with your bank ahead of time to see if they have partner banks or ATMs in Zurich where you may withdraw money without incurring extra fees. Using credit cards that do not impose international transaction fees might also save you money.

Remember to prepare ahead of time your money and to prioritize the activities and sites that are most essential to you. With careful preparation and these money-saving tips, you can make your vacation to Zurich more cheap while still having a good time.

Bargaining and Negotiation Strategies

Bargaining is not popular in Switzerland, especially at established retail businesses in cities like Zurich. However, there are a few things to bear in mind as a visitor in Zurich while making a purchase:

Price research: Before making a purchase, look into the typical price range for the item you wish to acquire. This will give you an idea of what to anticipate and assist you in determining if the price given is reasonable.

Visit local markets: While negotiating in shops may not be prevalent, you may find greater flexibility at local markets such as flea markets or outdoor markets. Some suppliers may be willing to negotiate in these situations, particularly if you're purchasing many things.

Discount: Instead of outright negotiating, you might enquire nicely about discounts or special deals. Inquire if there are any continuing deals, loyalty schemes, or price flexibility. Stores may sometimes feature specials or discounts that you are unaware of.

Buy in bulk: If you're purchasing numerous things from the same business, you may gently inquire about the potential of a discount when purchasing them all at once. As a show of goodwill, some shops may be ready to provide a little discount.

Consider cash payments: In certain circumstances, cash payments may provide a modest benefit by saving the merchant from credit card costs. While this does not guarantee a discount, it is worth considering if you are planning a large purchase.

Courteous manner: Throughout the procedure, it is critical to have a courteous and polite approach. Because Swiss society values professionalism and courtesy, being nice and thankful will benefit you.

Remember that negotiating is not established in Swiss society, so don't push too hard or get aggressive if your efforts fail. Enjoy your shopping in Zurich and concentrate on seeing the city's stunning attractions and local culture!

Zurich's Best Budget Markets

Zurich, Switzerland's biggest city, has a number of budget-friendly marketplaces where you may purchase a variety of things at reasonable costs. Here are some of Zurich's best budget markets:

Flohmarkt Kanzlei: Held on Saturdays in the Kanzleistrasse area, this flea market sells vintage clothes, antiques, furniture, books, and miscellaneous trinkets.

Helvetiaplatz Flea Market: This market, held every Saturday on Helvetiaplatz, contains a variety of second-hand products, vintage items, art, crafts, and food vendors. It's a terrific site to find one-of-a-kind products at low rates.

Bürkliplatz Market: On Tuesdays and Fridays, this open-air market runs along the picturesque Lake Zurich. It sells fresh vegetables, flowers, and plants, as well as regional delicacies like cheese, sausages, and baked products. Fresh ingredients may be purchased at low costs.

Oerlikon Market: This market, held on Wednesdays and Saturdays in Oerlikon, offers a wide variety of items such as fruits, vegetables, meat, fish, cheese, bread, and pastries. It's an excellent location for low-cost supermarket shopping.

Langstrasse Market: Held on Saturdays in Zurich's bustling Langstrasse area, this market provides a diverse variety of items. Clothing, accessories, crafts, artwork, and street food are all available at reasonable costs.

Sechseläutenplatz Market: This market, located near the Zurich Opera House, is open throughout the Christmas season. It has a variety of vendors offering gifts, decorations, food, and beverages. It's a great spot to go for cheap Christmas shopping.

These markets provide opportunities to learn about local culture, purchase inexpensive things, and interact with Zurich's colorful environment. Remember to double-check each market's working hours and exact dates, since they may change throughout the year.

Zurich Souvenirs

Zurich, Switzerland's biggest city, has a wide range of beautiful souvenirs that you may take home as a reminder of your stay. The following are some popular Zurich souvenirs:

Swiss Chocolate: Zurich, like the rest of Switzerland, is famous for its delectable chocolates. There is a large assortment of high-quality Swiss chocolates in a variety of flavors and styles. Brands to look for include Lindt, Sprüngli, and Toblerone.

Swiss Watches: Switzerland is well-known for its precise watches, and Zurich is home to a plethora of luxury watch manufacturers. Explore the city's watch stores and boutiques for superb Swiss timepieces that make excellent everlasting mementos.

Swiss Army Knife: The classic Swiss Army Knife is a multi-purpose tool originating in Switzerland. It is well-known for its toughness and usefulness. Zurich has a wide selection of Swiss Army Knives of various sizes and functions.

Swiss Cheese: Switzerland is well-known for its cheese manufacturing, and sampling some local Swiss cheese while in Zurich is a must. Look for Emmental, Gruyère, and Appenzeller cheeses. Cheese may be purchased in specialist stores or at local farmers' markets.

Swiss Souvenir timepieces: In addition to luxury timepieces, souvenir watches with Swiss themes or distinctive Swiss emblems are available. These timepieces are often less expensive and might serve as a distinctive and handy keepsake.

Swiss Cowbells: A pleasant and iconic memento, the classic Swiss cowbell. These bells, which Swiss cows use in the Alps, come in a variety of sizes and shapes. They make a lovely decoration or a one-of-a-kind gift.

Zurich provides a variety of textiles and materials that reflect Swiss workmanship. Look for Swiss needlework, lace, and traditional clothes such as Dirndls and Lederhosen. These textiles may be utilized for a variety of applications or displayed as ornamental items.

Swiss Artisanal items: There are various artisanal businesses in Zurich that sell locally manufactured crafts and items. Handcrafted products include ceramics, woodwork, glassware, and jewelry. These one-of-a-kind sculptures emphasize Swiss workmanship and make excellent keepsakes.

Swiss Posters & Prints: Zurich has a vibrant art culture, and there are stunning posters and prints featuring Swiss landscapes, cityscapes, and iconic artworks. These prints may be framed and exhibited as a memento of your Zurich vacation.

Swiss Wine: Although Switzerland is not as well-known for its wine as some other nations, it produces great wines. Consider buying a bottle of Swiss wine, especially from Zurich's neighboring vineyards, as a memento for wine lovers.

Remember to visit Zurich's local stores, marketplaces, and boutiques for even more one-of-a-kind gifts that encapsulate the soul of the city and Switzerland as a whole.

Zurich Safety Tips For Tourists

If you're visiting Zurich for the first time, you've chosen a lovely and bustling city to explore! Here are some safety precautions and recommendations to guarantee a safe and happy experience:

Personal Security:

Zurich is a safe city in general, but it's always a good idea to be vigilant and aware of your surroundings.

Keep your possessions safe and be wary of pickpockets, particularly in busy locations, public transit, and tourist sites.

Displaying costly products or big sums of money in public may draw unwelcome attention.

Transportation Security:

The public transit system in Zurich is efficient and dependable. To move about the city, use trams, buses, or trains.

Before boarding, make sure you have a valid ticket and remember to verify it. Fare evasion may lead to penalties.

When crossing the street, utilize marked pedestrian crossings wherever practical.

Emergency Preparedness

In an emergency, phone 112 for general assistance or 117 to contact the police.

Keep the address and phone number of your lodging accessible.

Water Security:

Zurich is located on the Limmat River and Lake Zurich. While swimming is permitted in specific spots, be aware of the current and heed any written cautions.

Consider using a life jacket while partaking in water sports if you are not a good swimmer.

Outdoor Recreation:

If you want to walk or visit the local mountains, make sure you're properly equipped, including strong footwear, weather-appropriate clothes, and enough food.

Before going on any outdoor excursions, check the weather and local rules.

Travel and health insurance:

Travel insurance that covers medical crises and other unexpected occurrences during your vacation is usually advised.

If you need medicine, make sure you bring enough and keep it in its original packaging.

Local Customs and Laws:

To prevent inadvertent violations, get acquainted with local laws and traditions.

While public alcohol use is largely tolerated, public drunkenness and unruly conduct may result in fines or legal penalties.

Tap Water

Zurich's tap water is of good quality and safe to drink. Carry a reusable water bottle with you throughout the day to remain hydrated.

Remember that these safety guidelines apply to most tourist places, and Zurich is recognized for having a low crime rate. You may have a safe and pleasant trip in this lovely city by exercising common sense and being aware of your surroundings.

Zurich Day Trip Excursions

If you're in Zurich and want to tour surrounding towns during the day, you have a few possibilities. Here are some popular places and how to get there:

Lucerne: About an hour from Zurich, Lucerne is a lovely town hidden in the Swiss Alps. From Zurich Hauptbahnhof (the major railway station), you may take a train to Lucerne. Trains travel often, and the route provides stunning scenery.

Winterthur: This cultural city is just about a 20-minute train journey away from Zurich. Winterthur is well-known for its thriving cultural scene, museums, and stunning gardens. Trains leave Zurich Hauptbahnhof on a regular basis.

Schaffhausen and the Rhine Falls: If you're looking for natural marvels, go to Schaffhausen and the Rhine Falls, Europe's biggest waterfall. You may take the train from Zurich to Schaffhausen, and then take a short bus journey to the Rhine Falls.

Baden is a historical town known for its warm springs and Roman remains. Trains run frequently from Zurich to Baden and take around 20 minutes. Baden is particularly well-known for its lovely gardens and picturesque old town.

The Swiss public transit system is your best hope for navigating these possibilities. The Swiss Federal Railways (SBB) maintain a large rail network that connects Zurich to surrounding municipalities. Trains are quick, comfortable, and provide breathtaking scenery along the route. You can check train timetables, plan your trip, and buy tickets online or at the railway station with ease.

Additionally, buses and trams are accessible throughout the towns, making it easy to see local sites. It's a good idea to double-check the transit choices and timetables for each location, since they may differ.

It's usually a good idea to organize your schedule ahead of time, consider the opening hours of the sites you want to see, and check for any potential closures or special events. This way, you may maximize your time and assure a pleasant and pleasurable journey from Zurich.

Websites and Resources For Zurich tourism

There are various useful websites that may give you vital information and tools if you are considering a vacation to Zurich, Switzerland. Here are some websites that might help you organize your trip and explore Zurich:

Official Zurich Tourism Website: The official Zurich Tourism website is a fantastic place to start. It provides detailed information on attractions, events, lodging, transportation, and other topics. Go to **https://www.zuerich.com**/ to learn more.

MySwitzerland.com: This website contains general information on Switzerland, especially Zurich. It provides information on prominent sights, activities, modes of transportation, and travel suggestions. Visit *https://www.myswitzerland.com/en-us/destinations/zurich/* to learn more about Zurich.

Zurich Public Transportation: The Zurcher Verkehrsverbund (ZVV) website offers information on public transportation alternatives in and around Zurich. There is information on trains, trams, buses, and boats, as well as timetables and fares. Their website may be found at *https://www.zvv.ch/zvv/en/home.html*.

Zurich Airport: If you're flying in, the official Zurich Airport website has information on flights, transportation to the city center, airport amenities, and more. Their website may be found at *https://www.zurich-airport.com/.*

TripAdvisor is a famous travel website that provides user reviews, suggestions, and advice for Zurich hotels, restaurants, sights, and activities. It may be a useful tool for locating the finest locations to visit and activities to do. To learn more about their Zurich vacation packages, go to *https://www.tripadvisor.com/Tourism-g188113-Zurich-Vacations.html.*

Zurich Museum Guide: Zurich is home to several museums, and the Zurich Museum Guide website provides information on the city's museums, including collections, opening hours, and special exhibits. Visit *https://www.museums.ch/* to learn more.

These websites should be a goldmine of information to help you plan your trip to Zurich and make the most of your stay there.

Conclusion

Finally, Zurich, with its rich history, breathtaking surroundings, and bustling city life, provides a genuinely unforgettable vacation experience. We have researched the city's myriad attractions, dug into its cultural and historical legacy, and discovered its hidden jewels throughout this guidebook.

Zurich's gorgeous position, perched on the shores of Lake Zurich and surrounded by snow-capped mountains, provides tourists with an enthralling background. Nature lovers will be immersed in a world of natural beauties, from the serene serenity of the lake to the stunning vistas from Uetliberg.

The city hums with life, flawlessly mixing its medieval heritage with contemporary architecture and a bustling cultural scene. Travelers will be charmed by Zurich's diverse cultural tapestry as they explore the cobblestone alleyways of the Old Town, browse through world-class museums, or attend one of the numerous festivals and events.

Zurich's culinary scene is a joy for foodies. The city's culinary offerings span from traditional Swiss delicacies to foreign cuisines. Visitors may taste the flavors of Zurich's gastronomic pleasures by eating at a comfortable café, indulging in gourmet restaurants, or visiting the busy food markets.

Furthermore, Zurich's excellent transit infrastructure makes navigating the city and venturing outside its limits a breeze. Day visits to surrounding sights, such as the majestic Rhine Falls or the attractive town of Lucerne, are easily accessible, adding to the options for exploration and discovery.

We have stressed Zurich's role as a worldwide financial center throughout our handbook. However, the city is not characterized exclusively by its economic strength. Residents of Zurich, noted for their warm hospitality and dedication to quality of life, help to create a welcome and inclusive environment for tourists from all walks of life.

Zurich, in summary, is a place that blends natural beauty, cultural legacy, and a vibrant metropolitan environment. Zurich offers something for everyone, whether you are a history buff, an art aficionado, an outdoor adventurer, or a foodie. This handbook is intended to be a companion, offering useful insights and ideas to guarantee a memorable and enlightening tour through this beautiful Swiss city. So pack your bags, immerse yourself in Zurich's allure, and brace yourself for an extraordinary experience that will leave you wanting to return again and again.

Printed in Great Britain
by Amazon